Dragon Chinese Horoscope 2025

By
IChingHunFùyǒu FengShuisu

Table of Contents

Introduce

The character of people born in the year of the DRAGON

People born this year are sexy, cute, agile, and charming, and whoever sees them loves them. Popular perfection is also available. People born in the Year of the Dragon are self-assured. You are dynamic, influential, and quick. You have a strong and steadfast personality as well. People born in the Year of the Dragon enjoy talking, often have strong opinions, enjoy advising others, and produce excellent work. They are, however, angry and self-satisfied. Self-assurance is so strong that it is easily irritated, stubborn, authoritarian, and snobbish. Obsessed with position and money. People born in this year only have lovers. Always have faith in love. If he were a woman, young men would come almost every day to flirt with him.

Strength:
You are courageous and ambitious.
Weaknesses:

You are stubborn, and direct, and tend to do things that are beyond your control.

Love:
People born this year will be preoccupied with finding a partner or selecting a lover. You're not interested in his social standing or family. People enjoy accepting who their lover is. They are, indeed, very romantic. It also has a fascinating love mood in the stage that is sweet, and soft, and people born this year are often flirting, but it is a quiet flirt. However, it is capable of effective restraint. If it's a woman, she might pick the ugliest man to be her boyfriend. Like anything unusual. Similarly, if she's a man, she'll pick a girl who no one likes as her boyfriend. Strangely, his actions can completely occupy the hearts of lovers. When you have feelings for someone. You're always worried about it. You take care of your lover and will never break his or her heart.

Suitable Career:
Because people born in the year of the Dragon are earth elementals. As a result, a profession

destined for people born with your element is suitable for jobs related to soil and land, such as real estate. Trading in jade, stone, farming, farming, horticulture, livestock, feed industry, fertilizer, building materials, brokers, or full-time jobs that do not require movements, such as company employees, clerks, secretaries, administrative personnel, etc.

Year of the DRAGON (Gold) | (1940) & (2000)

"The DRAGON Fly" is a person born in the year of the DRAGON at the age of 85 years (1940) and 25 years (2000)

Overview

For senior horoscopes, the planets that orbit your horoscope house this year are the "Jade Palace Star". At this age, you should get enough rest and take care of your health. Focus on hygiene and eating clean and appropriate for your age. Just be careful not to get dizzy or fall, which will cause injury or bleeding. The most important thing this year is not to get involved in your children's and grandchildren's affairs too much. You should act like a shelter for your children and grandchildren. This year, your children and grandchildren will love and care for you. Please be at ease and not stressed, which will make your life happy.

For horoscopes around the age of 25, this year is considered an auspicious year because many auspicious constellations are orbiting, which will cause bad things to turn into good things and heavy things to become light. You will have the opportunity to establish a foundation. Therefore, you should be diligent and constantly develop new skills to keep up with the ever-changing situation. If you work regularly or are a civil servant, this year your work will catch the eye of your elders and you will have the opportunity to be promoted. If you do your own business, this year you will be able to expand or your desired projects will take shape more. Finances will flow in heavily. Working together or investing in shares will be good, which will bring satisfying returns. However, there are important things that you should be careful about: Beware of envious people who may find ways to harm you, harass you, or harm you. Therefore, in an unfavorable month, you should take care of your work and responsibilities as best you can. Try not to argue back and do not be arrogant about your abilities. On days when you have power or are superior, think of others' feelings and be kind in your life. Do not think of bullying those who are inferior to you. Your life will only find happiness.

Career and Business

This year is another year with a chance of progress, whether in your career, studies, or business because you will find someone to help you. Therefore, it is considered a golden year for work. You have the opportunity to do business or open your own business. If you have a regular job, you have the opportunity to be promoted. However, you must improve your interpersonal skills with both your superiors and subordinates. You must always be humble, not show off your skills, and give importance to your subordinates. You should also be open to listening to opinions from all sides. Although the stars give you auspicious power, success will not happen if you are not diligent, do not know how to seize opportunities, and just stay in the same place. Therefore, you should use this good opportunity this year to quickly improve your skills to do a second or third part-time job. This will help you save money for the future. In terms of collaboration and investment, this year has a good direction. You will receive support and investment will receive beautiful returns. The months when your work and investment will be very good are the 2nd Chinese month (March 5 – April 3), the 3rd Chinese month (April 4 – May 4), the 6th Chinese month (July 7 – August 6), and the 10th Chinese month (November 7 – December 6).

The months when your work will be obstructed and have problems are the 1st Chinese month (February 3 – March 4), the 4th Chinese month (May 5 – June 4), the 8th Chinese month (September 7 – October 7), and the 9th Chinese month (October 8 – November 6). When accepting work, giving orders, and doing work, please do not do it carelessly. You should pay attention to following the existing rules and regulations and the correct methods. When drafting legally binding contracts, you should consider the details that may unknowingly lead to being taken advantage of.

Financial

This year, your financial luck is moderate. Income from salary or sales of goods or services will flow normally. However, if you hope for an unexpected windfall, you must be mindful and not be greedy because gambling will have both wins and losses. In particular, in the months when your financial luck is low, there will be problems and unexpected expenses, namely, the 1st Chinese month (February 3 - March 4), the 4th Chinese month (May 5 - June 4), the 8th Chinese month (September 7 - October 7), and the 9th Chinese month (October 8 - November 6). Do not lend money to others or accept guarantees. Do not invest in businesses that are at risk of breaking the law. Be careful of dangers from scammers. The months when your finances flow smoothly are the 2nd Chinese month (5 March – 3 April), the 3rd Chinese month (4 April – 4 May), the 6th Chinese month (7 July – 6 August), and the 10th Chinese month (7 November – 6 December).

Family

This year is an auspicious time to move into a new house and there will be good fortune and good things to be happy about. Family members will have good fortune and prosperity. For senior horoscopes, living with children in the house, you should close one eye and not interfere with children's matters. Then, you will be loved by your children. For horoscopes around the age of 25, this year is considered a year of good fortune in the family. Family members will love each other well. There will be no problems for you to worry about. However, during the 1st Chinese month (February 3 - March 4), the 4th Chinese month (May 5 - June 4), the 8th Chinese month (September 7 - October 7), and the 9th Chinese month (October 8 - November 6), you should be careful of accidents in the house. Valuable property may be damaged or stolen. Be careful of family members quarreling with outsiders because this year there is a chance that someone will cause trouble. Therefore, you should help to prevent people in the house and try to avoid quarrels to make the house peaceful.

Love

For senior people, you should not be picky with your children and grandchildren. You will be respected and loved by your children and grandchildren in your home. For young people in their 25th year, this year, love will be sweet. You will be well taken care of by the opposite sex or your lover. If you are ready or have made up your mind, this year there will be an auspicious date for engagement, marriage, or moving out. For those who do not have a lover, this year there is a chance to meet someone you like. However, you will have to study each other thoroughly to weave a relationship from friends to lovers. Especially for those who are single, the people you meet this year are likely to be the real deal. Please consider dating them carefully before sharing a bed. However, both age groups should be careful during the months when your love will have problems, which are the 1st Chinese month (February 3 – March 4), the 4th Chinese month (May 5 – June 4), the 8th Chinese month (September 7 – October 7), and the 9th Chinese month (October 8 – November 6). During this period, there is a chance that there will be arguments. Therefore, you should not interfere in other people's family matters. You should also know how to protect yourself if you have to go to entertainment venues. Because there may be freebies included.

Health

For the elderly, your general health is normal. Please take good care of your health and be careful about your food and hygiene. The food you eat should be easy to digest and not too spicy. Be careful when walking or you might get dizzy and fall, which could be dangerous. Therefore, when you go anywhere, you should have someone close to you. For young people, you are healthy this year. However, during the

1st Chinese Month (February 3 – March 4), the 4th Chinese Month (May 5 – June 4), the 8th Chinese Month (September 7 – October 7), and the 9th Chinese Month (October 8 – November 6), you must be careful of illnesses, especially gastritis, enteritis, and food poisoning. You should not drive after drinking alcohol. You must also be careful of accidents while working and traveling. Please do not be careless.

Year of the DRAGON (Water) | (1952) & (2012)

" The DRAGON swam in the rain " is a person born in the year of the DRAGON at the age of 73 years (1952) and 13 years (2012)

Overview

For senior horoscope people aged 73, this year is another year that will experience auspicious power in the family. You will have the opportunity to buy expensive property. There is a chance to organize an auspicious event for your children. You will have the opportunity to make merit donate money to public charities or help with social work with your children. This merit-making will help enhance your children's reputation and make them well-known. It will also promote your children's career or business. Although the power of auspicious stars will help promote progress in careers and business, there are also bad stars in your horoscope that will harass you. Therefore, things will not go smoothly. You must be careful about health problems and accidents. Be careful when walking or you will get dizzy and fall. You should also avoid nagging your children or grandchildren. Be careful not to argue. For children aged 13, this year the power of auspicious power will help your studies progress. However, it does not mean that you are lazy and will not succeed if you do not put in the effort. Therefore, you should be diligent and review your studies. Do not show off. Your studies will have good grades and progress to another level. In addition, you should be careful not to cause trouble with naughty children. Also, avoid various temptations that will cause you to lose concentration in your studies. Therefore, you should divide your play time and study time well. And you should know how to distinguish between friends. Be careful not to be deceived. When you have a problem, you should ask for advice from a trusted adult, rather than consulting with friends.

Career and Business

For business and education, this year, due to the auspicious stars orbiting to promote progress and prosperity, it is a good opportunity for you. If you do a lot this year, you will be able to increase sales, expand your customer base, and increase production capacity. The more you do, the more chances you will have to earn money. For students, because there are auspicious stars that support and support education, if combined with determination and diligence, it is believed that there will be a chance to get good grades, whether in educational competitions or even score top in a certain subject. And will be admired by parents and teachers. In particular, the months when your work and study will have a bright and prosperous direction are the 2nd Chinese month (5 March – 3 April), the 3rd Chinese month (4 April – 4 May), the 6th Chinese month (7 July – 6 August), and the 10th Chinese month (7 November – 6 December). However, you should be careful during the months when your work will be hindered and have problems, which are the 1st Chinese month (3 February – 4 March), the 4th Chinese month (5 May – 4 June), the 8th Chinese month (7 September – 7 October), and the 9th Chinese month (8 October – 6 November). Be careful of making contracts that you may be deceived and taken advantage of. You should also avoid making any investments during the aforementioned months.

Financial

This year, your financial fortune is quite good. There will be income from many channels. Even though it seems like you have to rotate money around dizzyingly, in the end, you will have enough to spend. During the year, your seniors may assign their heirs or assistants to help look after external investments. There is a tendency for good returns, especially during the months when your finances flow smoothly, such as the 2nd Chinese month (March 5 – April 3), the 3rd Chinese month (April 4 – May 4), the 6th Chinese month (July 7 – August 6), and the 10th Chinese month (November 7 – December 6). As for the months when your finances will be disrupted, Including unexpected expenses that may occur in the following months: the 1st Chinese month (February 3 - March 4), the 4th Chinese month (May 5 - June 4), the 8th Chinese month (September 7 - October 7), and the 9th Chinese month (October 8 - November). Do not lend money to others or sign financial guarantees. Do not gamble with the hope of getting a windfall and do not invest in illegal businesses. There is a chance of injury or loss, or you may be deceived by criminals.

Family

Family: Although this year there will be auspicious energy visiting the house, there will be misfortune from the younger ones causing trouble. You should also be careful about the safety of your family members. While talking and exchanging ideas, you should not be emotional with each other. Even if some members accidentally do something wrong or do not go as you wish, you should forgive them. Otherwise, small things may escalate into big problems and cause problems later. In particular, the months when family members will experience problems and chaos are the Chinese 1st month (February 3 – March 4), the 4th Chinese month (May 5 – June 4), the 8th Chinese month (September 7 – October 7), and the 9th Chinese month (October 8 – November 6). You must be careful about accidents in the house. Be careful about family members arguing. Be careful about valuables being damaged, lost, or falling victim to criminals.

For young people in this age group, be careful about friends inviting you to hang out in groups. There will be misfortune and injury.

Love

Love in the first 6 months will be smooth. In the second half of the year, arguments and conflicts will easily occur. The most important thing you should be careful about is to try not to bring up past mistakes. This will cause anger to flare up again. Arguing in front of your children will cause them to lose faith. The months when your love is fragile and arguments will easily occur are the 1st Chinese month (February 3 - March 4), the 4th Chinese month (May 5 - June 4), the 8th Chinese month (September 7 - October 7), and the 9th Chinese month (October 8 - November 6). You should not interfere or interfere in other people's family matters. You should also avoid going to entertainment venues.

Health

The health of both horoscopes this year is in good condition because the horoscope houses have the auspicious stars "Tikoi" (the Earth Correcting Star) and "Leng Tek" (the Virtuous Dragon Star), which both stars will help promote good health. If sick, it will help find the hypothesis of the disease or find a good doctor with good medicine that can cure the illness quickly. However, if you notice anything unusual early, you should see a doctor for treatment from the beginning of symptoms because there is a higher chance of being cured. However, you should be careful during the months when you need to take close care of your health, which are the 1st Chinese month (February 3 – March 4), the 4th Chinese month (May 5 – June 4), the 8th Chinese month (September 7 – October 7), and the 9th Chinese month (October 8 – November 6). Be careful of injuries from accidents, joint pain, and continuous headaches.

Year of the DRAGON (Fire) | (1964)

" The Dragon in Ocean" is a person born in the year of the DRAGON at the age of 61 years (1964)

Overview

For those who are 61 years old, this year, whether it is your career or business, you will progress. The days and times of the Year of the Snake 2025 are quite smooth and prosperous. Therefore, it is a good opportunity for you to accelerate your work, increase sales, expand your customer base, or increase your production. It would not be wrong to say that this is your golden year. Therefore, please maintain diligence and continuously develop and add new skills to yourself. Do not let time pass by without doing anything. However, during this year, there will be an evil star that will disturb your horoscope house, which will result in conflicts and arguments, and only chaotic things that will cause you headaches. Therefore, you should be careful or have a backup plan to solve problems when difficult things happen.

Career and Business

This year, your career will find a sponsor. Therefore, your career and business will have a path of progress. You will have the opportunity to expand your work and open additional branches. It is also a good time to look for children or representatives to take over the work or plan to expand your work, expand your business or expand your production, expand your sales, and apply it this year. Use your intelligence and diligence to push your plan to become a reality. Under smooth times, when combined with your abilities, it will help you to be wealthy and able to step towards success.

Especially during the months when your career and business progress well, namely, the 2nd Chinese month (March 5 - April 3), the 3rd Chinese month (April 4 - May 4), the 6th Chinese month (July 7 - August 6), and the 10th Chinese month (November 7 - December 6). In addition, both internal and external investments during this period will be satisfactory returns. However, during the 1st Chinese month (Feb 3 – Mar 4), 4th Chinese month (May 5 – June 4), 8th Chinese month (Sep 7 – Oct 7), and 9th Chinese month (Oct 8 – Nov 6), be careful of insiders betraying you or falsifying your accounts, causing damage. Also, when changing job positions, be careful of conflicts. You should assign the right people to the right jobs. Don't choose them because they are close friends or personal acquaintances. This will make others feel that the flatterer is doing well, which will cause division and undermine the morale of those who are dedicated to their work. Therefore, please conduct yourself well, closely monitor your accounts, and avoid any investments during these periods.

Financial

This year, your financial horoscope will have a better income than last year. Money will flow in from many sources from the things you have invested and worked hard for, including money from luck. In addition, both internal and external investments are also bright and will have satisfactory returns. The months when your finances will flow smoothly are the 2nd

Chinese month (March 5 - April 3), the 3rd Chinese month (April 4 - May 4), the 6th Chinese month (July 7 - August 6), and the 10th Chinese month (November 7 - December 6). However, you should be careful during the months when your finances will be stuck and unexpectedly incur expenses, which are the 1st Chinese month (February 3 - March 4), the 4th Chinese month (May 5 - June 4), the 8th Chinese month (September 7 - October 7), and the 9th Chinese month (October 8 - November 6). Do not lend money and accept guarantees. Do not engage in any illegal business and do not gamble.

Family

This year, the family horoscope is moderate. Even if there are some conflicts, just stay calm and you will be able to successfully bring peace and tranquility back to your family. As the saying goes, harmony brings good fortune to your home. Don't be a stingy person, or make small things into big things. Do things that can be forgiven or forgiven, even if you have to force yourself, but the matter will end.

However, you should be careful during the months when there will be problems and conflicts within your family, which are: 1st Chinese Month (February 3 – March 4), 4th Chinese Month (May 5 – June 4), 8th Chinese Month (September 7 – October 7), and 9th Chinese Month (October 8 – November 6). Be careful of people in the house or your subordinates getting into arguments with outsiders. You should also take care of your home's safety, electrical systems, and fixtures. If you see any, you should repair them immediately to return them to good condition. Also, be careful of dangers from criminals.

Love

This year, love is moderate. You will have the opportunity to travel with your lover and family members on a long-distance trip or visit distant relatives. This will happen during the 1st Chinese Month (February 3 – March 4), 4th Chinese Month (May 5 – June 4), 8th Chinese Month (September 7 – October 7), and 9th Chinese Month (October 8 – November 6). Be careful of arguing with your partner or lover due to instigation from others. You must keep your mind steady and not be shaken by words that you do not see with your own eyes or hear with your ears. In doing anything, do not be self-centered and think that you are the only one who is right. In addition, do not interfere in other people's family matters. Also, do not go to entertainment venues. Be careful of bringing back illnesses.

Health

Your health this year is not good. Be careful of stress or insufficient rest that will cause illness. Be careful of high blood pressure, gastritis, enteritis, diabetes, and food poisoning. This year, you have to be especially strict about what you eat. You should avoid cold foods and foods that are very spicy, whether sweet, fatty, or salty. The months when you have to take more care of your health are the 1st Chinese month (February 3 – March 4), the 4th Chinese month (May 5 – June 4), the 8th Chinese month (September 7 – October 7), and the 9th Chinese month (October 8 – November 6). The person should be more careful because insufficient rest can cause high blood pressure, which will easily cause accidents. Therefore, if you feel dizzy or lightheaded, you should see a doctor immediately. Find time to take care of your body more. Most importantly, you have to let go of some things. While working with machines or sitting behind the wheel, you must not be careless about accidents.

Year of the DRAGON (Earth) | (1976)

" The DRAGON in Heaven" is a person born in the year of the DRAGON at the age of 49 years (1976)

Overview

For the Dragon horoscope in this age group, even though the unsmoothness from last year has decreased, this year is still a period in which you cannot act hastily or hastily, because you may encounter mistakes and damages. You should not be careless with any activities because there are groups of evil stars orbiting to harass your horoscope house. This group of inauspicious stars often affects conflicts, disputes, betrayal, business scheming, corruption, and arguments. Therefore, you should prepare yourself to cope with it. However, you are lucky because there will be auspicious stars to help and support you many times. In addition to the "Jimui Star" that shines the light, there is also the "Tee Koi Star" (the Earth Correcting Star) orbiting to shine aura to help amidst the circle of dark energy, helping to relieve and ease from severe to mild. You should also be careful of problems that will affect your health, especially frequent headaches, migraines, or abnormal blood pressure. You should therefore fix this by getting enough rest and controlling your diet. Whether it is sweet, fatty, or salty, don't let it be too spicy, as it will cause excess fat to accumulate or affect your digestive system, waste filtration in the body, and cause high blood sugar, etc. This year, in addition to taking care of your physical health, another important thing that you cannot neglect is accidents. If you are physically exhausted, do not work that requires using tools or machinery or drive a vehicle because you may have an accident and get injured.

Career and Business
This year's career criteria are quite unstable, and there are often storms of problems. Therefore, before moving forward or doing any work, you should plan carefully and thoroughly, have a backup plan to cope with sudden changes, and always be prepared in various aspects to cope with them. What cannot be avoided this year are conflicts, protests, and being betrayed, especially in unfavorable months. In terms of work and trade, mistakes and problems can easily occur, such as the 1st Chinese month (February 3 - March 4), the 4th Chinese month (May 5 - June 4), the 8th Chinese month (September 7 - October 7), and the 9th Chinese month (October 8 - November 6). Starting a new job, and entering into a joint venture, including internal and external investments are criteria to watch out for, and you must analyze the surrounding factors carefully. If you stubbornly invest in a joint venture during a time that is not conducive, it

will only lead to arguments and disputes, causing you to not look at each other. You should also be more careful in your work. Take care and be fair to your subordinates or those under your command equally. When making any contracts, be careful of hidden details and beware of greed that will make you a victim of fraud, causing damage and loss of property. The months when your work or business will have a bright and prosperous direction are the 2nd Chinese month (March 5 – April 3), the 3rd Chinese month (April 4 – May 4), the 6th Chinese month (July 7 – August 6), and the 10th Chinese month (November 7 – December 6).

Financial

Finance Direct income from salary and overall sales are decreasing. Special income is still uncertain and if you hope for money from gambling, it will be very risky. You should also take good care of your cash flow management, especially during the months when your finances will be stuck, lack liquidity, and financial leaks, which are the 1st Chinese month (February 3 - March 4), the 4th Chinese month (May 5 - June 4), the 8th Chinese month (September 7 - October 7) and the 9th Chinese month (October 8 - November 6). During these periods, you should not gamble. Do not lend money to others or sign financial guarantees. Do not invest in illegal businesses. The months when your finances will flow smoothly are the 2nd Chinese month (March 5 - April 3), the 3rd Chinese month (April 4 - May 4), the 6th Chinese month (July 7 - August 6) and the 10th Chinese month (November 7 - December 6).

Family

This year, the family horoscope of this person is rather lacking in peace. You should be careful of unexpected incidents that will cause chaos and trouble in your home. In particular, you should be careful of safety problems, accidents, and health problems of people in your home who may suffer injuries or bleeding, especially during the months when your family will be in trouble and conflicts will easily occur, such as the 1st Chinese month (February 3 - March 4), the 4th Chinese month (May 5 - June 4), the 8th Chinese month (September 7 - October 7), and the 9th Chinese month (October 8 - November 6). The person should pay more attention to the health of people in the home. Be careful of valuables in the home being lost, damaged, or cheated by scammers. For close friends and relatives, this year is in the middle range. However, you cannot be quick-tempered and quick-witted. Sometimes, if you offend or taunt others, you may feel that it is a joke and not serious, but the person you are mentioning will feel embarrassed. Be careful not to be naughty and have fun, as it may turn into accumulating resentment and waiting for the day you get your revenge. Therefore, you should not find more enemies. Always keep your mouth shut and think before you speak, it will be safer.

Love

This year, the love of this person will face many storms because, in the horoscope house, evil stars are rolling their tongues to disturb and aim at the base of love. Therefore, there will often be arguments that destroy the peace. Be careful of arguing and causing a big problem from a trivial matter, just because you are easily overheard and overheard by others without thinking and examining the cause. You should be careful during the months when your love is quite fragile and will easily cause arguments and quarrels, namely the 1st Chinese month (February 3 - March 4), the 4th Chinese month (May 5 - June 4), the 8th Chinese month (September 7 - October 7), and the 9th Chinese month (October 8 - November 6). However, you should avoid the triggers that will easily cause arguments by avoiding going to entertainment venues and not getting involved in other people's family matters. Also, be careful of saying things that will hurt your partner's feelings.

Health

This year, health should not be neglected. Be careful of minor illnesses but do not seek treatment immediately as they will escalate into major problems. In addition, your body this year seems to be quite weak from many things that have come together at the same time. Also, you do not get enough rest, causing your immunity to diseases to decline. Illnesses will attack and make you sick easily. Also, be careful of eating and drinking whatever you want as it will undermine your health because you are getting old. Eating foods high in fat may cause high cholesterol in the blood vessels. Eating too much salty food may cause high blood pressure. Therefore, you should be careful of these things. Especially during the months when you need to take close care of your health, which are the 1st Chinese month (February 3 - March 4), the 4th Chinese month (May 5 - June 4), the 8th Chinese month (September 7 - October 7), and the 9th Chinese month (October 8 - November 6). During the aforementioned months, when traveling near or far, including working with tools and machines, you should be careful of accidents. If you feel anything unusual in your body, see a doctor immediately for diagnosis and treatment.

Year of the DRAGON (Wood) | (1988)

" The Dragon In Ocean" is a person born in the year of the DRAGON at the age of 37 years (1988)

Overview

For those born in the year of the Dragon, this year is another auspicious year in which you will find a patron. Your career will show a path of progress. Your business will flourish. Both auspicious stars will help your work go smoothly. If you are an employee in a company or organization or a civil servant, this year you will be considered for a position adjustment or salary increase. Therefore, you should work with determination, always research, and develop new skills for yourself. Your boss will see your goodness and abilities. For those who do their own business or do business, this year sales will expand. If there is a good opportunity, you can agree to accept a big job because this year you will have a high power of success. However, for any big work this year to be successful, you will need cooperation from your colleagues. Therefore, the main factor this year is to have good human relations with people around you. Your work will be as prosperous as hoped. However, you should be careful because, during the year, there will be a group of bad stars orbiting in your horoscope house, which will cause conflicts, arguments, being deceived, or being hated or slandered by others. Although this year your work and business will still receive trust and cooperation from your friends, if you feel irritated or aggressive, you should be careful not to take your emotions out on anyone. Including reducing arrogance and pride, because people close to you may withdraw their support, which will cause your work and business to be hindered and have obstacles instead. You should maintain humility at all times. Having good friendships and strengthening relationships with people at both the top and bottom levels will help push you to achieve success and progress, even more, this year.

Career and Business

This year, even though there is progress, you should not be impatient. You should build good relationships with those you have to do business with. You should also visit your customers often. At the same time, you should maintain good human relations with both your boss and subordinates to prevent people from being jealous and making you enemies. The months when your work has a good direction of progress and prosperity are the 2nd Chinese month (March 5 - April 3), the 3rd Chinese month (April 4 - May 4), the 6th Chinese month (July 7 - August 6), and the 10th Chinese month (November 7 - December 6). During these periods, starting a new job, entering into shares, and investing in various external investments will have satisfactory results. However, you should be careful during the months when your work will decline and problems will occur, namely, the 1st Chinese month (February 3 - March 4), the 4th Chinese month (May 5 - June 4), the 8th Chinese month (September 7 - October 7), and the 9th Chinese month (October 8 - November 6). When making a contract or hiring, you must carefully consider the details so that there will be no damage. Also, be careful of conflicts arising from transfers or job changes that may make some people unhappy. Also, during this period, you should avoid investing because there is a chance of being deceived. Also, be careful of dishonest people.

Financial

Your financial horoscope is good. Cash flow from salary or sales will flow continuously. For special money or windfall, if it falls during a favorable month, grab it quickly. However, you should not invest heavily or invest in high-risk things. Follow the motto "Greed often leads to lost fortune." In particular, the months when your finances will be stuck and you should be careful of unexpected expenses are the 1st Chinese month (February 3 – March 4), the 4th Chinese month (May 5 – June 4), the 8th Chinese month (September 7 – October 7), and the 9th Chinese month (October 8 – November 6). Do not lend money to others or act as a guarantor for anyone. Do not gamble or take risks. Do not invest in businesses that evade the law to save money and prevent you from suffering later. However, this year there are several months when you will have luck with money, namely the 2nd Chinese month (5 March – 3 April), the 3rd Chinese month (4 April – 4 May), the 6th Chinese month (7 July – 6 August) and the 10th Chinese month (7 November – 6 December).

Family

This year, due to the auspicious star of wealth, your home will likely organize an auspicious event or have the opportunity to move into a new home. For some, you will be able to build your status to be respected or credible in business transactions, such as buying a new car, opening a new store, or expanding a branch. However, if you enter the 1st Chinese Month (February 3 – March 4), the 4th Chinese Month (May 5 – June 4), the 8th Chinese Month (September 7 – October 7), and the 9th Chinese Month (October 8 – November 6), you must be careful of accidents that may happen to people in the home. Be careful of arguments among family members. Be careful of losing valuables or becoming a victim of fraud. Be careful of subordinates or juniors in the home who may have arguments with neighbors. Furthermore, do not get involved in conflicts between friends, especially those that may lead to lawsuits. Be careful of being tricked by friends to cause trouble and loss of property.

Love

This year, you and your lover will change their minds. Otherwise, you will often act in a way that does not match your heart. Even though you know that you love someone, your mouth often says different things, which can easily lead to arguments and deception even though you do not want to do it. Therefore, you should be patient and think carefully before speaking. In addition, you must be careful of a third party that may create problems and cause a rift in your relationship. You must make a good decision and do not let your emotions override your responsibility and morality. Bad things will turn into good things. Entering the 1st Chinese Month (February 3 - March 4), the 4th Chinese Month (May 5 - June 4), the 8th Chinese Month (September 7 - October 7), and the 9th Chinese Month (October 8 - November 6), you must avoid interfering in other people's family matters and be careful of arguing with your lover. In addition, you should not go to entertainment venues. Be careful not to fall into the trap of love that has been dug for you, which will cause you trouble and loss of wealth.

Health

This year, your health horoscope is moderately good. Be careful of exhaustion from work to the point of lack of sufficient rest. Also, too many parties that cause you to lose consciousness will cause accidents. In particular, the months when you need to take close care of your health are the 1st Chinese month (February 3rd - March 4th), the 4th Chinese month (May 5th - June 4th), the 8th Chinese month (September 7th - October 7th), and the 9th Chinese month (October 8th - November 6th). When using the road, be careful not to be careless and be careful not to get hit by other people's accidents. When going out to work outside the home, be careful of unexpected events that may cause you to be injured or bleed. Therefore, if you have to work in a risky area, you should wear a helmet or protective clothing first. If you work with tools or tanks that use pressure, be extra careful to reduce the severity.

Chinese Astrology Horoscope for Each Month

Month 12 in the Dragon Year (5 Jan 25 - 2 Feb 25)

Your horoscope this month is highly volatile. Some major problems are still lingering this month and cannot be resolved. You will also encounter obstacles and difficulties in negotiations that are not smooth. Your work and business are like coming across a test. You will encounter obstacles and may be scrutinized. Plan and prepare yourself to deal with them well. However, if you can get through this, you will be recognized for your skills. The most important thing you should do during this period is to do your work as best as you can. Do not interfere with other people's work. Behave appropriately and maintain humility. Do not rush your work. Communicate clearly before doing anything so that mistakes do not happen.

Your finances this month are quite abundant and will not cause you to worry. However, if you hope to earn money from gambling, be careful not to be greedy or you will fall victim to fraudsters. Investments are in good shape.

Your family will love and reconcile well this month. There will be good news in the home. There may be an auspicious event or you may move into a new house or open a new shop.

In terms of love, it is easy to argue and argue. Please remember that love must be honest and sincere. The presence of a third person may distract you. Therefore, please be mindful and restrain yourself. Also, be careful when visiting entertainment venues because you may catch a disease as a bonus.

There is nothing to worry about in terms of health.

Support Days: 3 Jan., 7 Jan., 11 Jan., 15 Jan., 19 Jan., 23 Jan., 27 Jan., 31 Jan.
Lucky Days: 4 Jan., 16 Jan., 28 Jan.
Misfortune Days: 5 Jan., 17 Jan., 29 Jan.
Bad Days: 8 Jan., 10 Jan., 20 Jan., 22 Jan.

Month 1 in the Snake Year (3 Feb 25 - 4 Mar 25)
This month, the road of life for those born in the year of the Horse moves to the destroyer line, which negative energy will affect the financial base of the person. Therefore, there will be unexpected large expenses or business will be interfered with by external crises, which will affect you as well. In terms of work and business during this period, even though there are many problems and obstacles, if you have good relationships with your colleagues and those you have to do business with all the time, the problems will be resolved from serious to light. When many heads work together to help each other, there will be a way out of the problem. The important thing you should do during this period is to cut out unnecessary and extravagant expenses. Avoid gambling, stocks, or gold. Also, do not be greedy for ill-gotten gains.

Avoid prolonging things to reduce conflicts. If a problem arises, you should fix it immediately. Do not let it escalate.

The family is peaceful, but be careful of losing valuables, damaging them, or being stolen. As for relatives, be careful with your words. Talking too much is not beneficial. Also, do not interfere in the internal affairs of your friends.

This month, your financial luck will face a storm. Expenses will catch up with your income, so you should plan and manage your liquidity well. Do not risk investing in things you are not skilled in and have high risks.

For love, there is freshness and brightness. It is a time when the tree of love blossoms beautifully. You should use this time to take good care of each other. And if you agree, you can talk about marriage proposals or marriage proposals, which are both auspicious times.

Support Days: 4 Feb., 8 Feb., 12 Feb., 16 Feb., 20 Feb., 24 Feb., 28 Feb.
Lucky Days: 9 Feb., 21 Feb.
Misfortune Days: 10 Feb., 22 Feb.
Bad Days: 1 Feb., 3 Feb., 13 Feb., 15 Feb., 25 Feb., 27 Feb.

Month 2 in the Snake Year (5 Mar 25 - 3 Apr 25)
This month marks the beginning of the Chinese New Year. It is another good opportunity for you to prepare yourself by planning and setting directions in various aspects, including planning your investment so that your work can proceed as efficiently as possible. You should also review past mistakes, what are your weaknesses that should be fixed, what are your strengths that should be used, start over, make improvements, and fill yourself with new skills that need to keep up with the changing situations this year.

In terms of work or business, during this period you will find a sponsor to give you advice. Investing in the foreign market is another path to future advancement. As for starting a new job, you will meet both good friends who will help you and bad friends who will try to destroy you or stab you in the back. Therefore, you should use your mind to analyze and distinguish. This month, you can invest in stocks and investments in various areas.

This month, your finances will be sufficient to make a living but be careful of family accidents in the home, and family members may argue. Be careful of thoughtless words that will lead to arguments among family members, especially problems caused by subordinates.

This is a good time for your lover to pay respects to the gods and ask for blessings. To make merit together, in terms of health, you should avoid food that causes heat in the body, such as fried or grilled food, because it will cause the body to have an excess of fire elements, lacking balance, causing illnesses. You should also be careful of accidents while using vehicles on the road.

Support Days: 4 Mar, 8 Mar., 12 Mar., 16 Mar., 20 Mar., 24 Mar., 28 Mar.
Lucky Days: 5 Mar, 17 Mar., 29 Mar.
Misfortune Days: 6 Mar, 18 Mar., 30 Mar.
Bad Days: 9 Mar., 11 Mar., 21 Mar., 23 Mar.

Month 3 in the Snake Year (4 Apr 25 - 4 May 25)
This month, your life path is in a better direction. Although problems from work or business remain, chaos is starting to ease up. However, you should not be so happy that you become careless. Always remember that only patience and diligence will help you get through this crisis. Therefore, you should use this opportunity to quickly resolve the problems that have been pending in the past period. Create and strengthen good relationships with those who have to contact both inside and outside the organization. Hurry to seize the good limited time, create results, and expand sales and income to accumulate capital for the future.

This month, your finances are quite good. It is a good time for both internal and external investments, which will receive returns. There will also be new income to increase liquidity.

In terms of work, you will find a patron and receive help. Therefore, you should use this opportunity to increase your diligence. It is like having two forces to help you. You will be able to create twice as much work. This will make your work outstanding and more successful.

This month, your family's horoscope is peaceful. There are also good times for moving and good news about auspicious events.

In terms of love, it is also in line with each other. There will be a good time for engagement, marriage, or moving out of the house. Or some people will meet someone they have been waiting for.

However, your health is in a state of exhaustion and fatigue. You have a chance to get sick without realizing it. Therefore, you should get enough rest, relax your mind, and take care of your hygiene. Be careful not to get sick with food poisoning.

Support Days: 1 Apr., 5 Apr., 9 Apr., 13 Apr., 17 Apr., 21 Apr., 25 Apr., 29 Apr.
Lucky Days: 10 Apr., 22 Apr.
Misfortune Days: 11 Apr., 23 Apr.

Bad Days: 2 Apr., 4 Apr., 14 Apr., 16 Apr., 26 Apr., 28 Apr.

Month 4 in the Snake Year (5 May 25 - 4 Jun 25)

This month, your horoscope will encounter obstacles and there will be a bad star orbiting to disturb you. There will be obstacles in your work and business. You should remember not to interfere in other people's matters and speak little to avoid conflicts. This is because you will encounter chaos in both your supervisory and general management work. Therefore, you must know how to use good interpersonal skills at both the top and bottom, of your subordinates. You must know how to compromise and use your mind to solve problems. The most important thing you should do during this period is to manage within your budget and ability. Do not create debts or be greedy for investment projects that others have drawn up to tempt you. Be careful not to fall for flattery or persuasion to make money improperly. This will only create more serious problems for yourself.

This month, your finances will be low with excessive expenses. Do not gamble or take risks. Do not invest in illegal businesses. Be careful of lawsuits. During this period, you should closely follow up on your debtors, be careful of bad debts, and be careful of making contracts with various obligations. This will cause you damage. Do not be careless.

For your family, be careful of accidents and take good care of your valuables in your home. You must also be careful not to fall victim to scammers.

For love, this is the time to dare to open your heart. If you want to say I love you, you should do it quickly because you will get a good response.

However, in terms of health, you still have to be careful of accidents during travel and be careful of high blood pressure, diabetes, and injuries and bleeding. You should always pay attention to hygiene when drinking and eating.

Support Days: 3 May, 7 May, 11 May, 15 May, 19 May, 23 May, 27 May, 31 May.
Lucky Days: 4 May, 16 May, 28 May.
Misfortune Days: 5 May, 17 May, 29 May.
Bad Days: 8 May, 10 May, 20 May, 22 May

Month 5 in the Snake Year (6 Jun 25 - 6 Jul 25)
This month, the horoscope of those born in the year of the Horse shows a positive energy line. Your life path will soar. Your work will progress and your business will flourish. This is also a good time and opportunity to expand your business, increase investment, or accelerate the creation of work results. The important thing you should do on this occasion is to find in-depth information about your work or business that you are taking care of. You must also go out to explore the market and observe the changing needs of consumers, and new technologies that you must always know how to develop and improve to keep up with your work and understand the market. If you have time, you should study the direction of new trade and investment markets. You should also

know how to make short-term and long-term payments to know when to hold on and when to let go.

This month, your financial luck is bright. Direct income and windfall income will come in continuously.

Your work still has a supporting force that will not fall. Your boss will help promote you and your subordinates will help support you. Strike while the iron is hot, so you have a chance to be promoted or expand your business opportunities. Starting a new job, joining a joint venture, and investing in various projects can be done.

For families, there are still good things to be happy about. There will be criteria for moving into a new place of work and there will be an auspicious date for work.

In terms of love, it is sweet and a time for the fruition of love. In addition, this period also has a good date for engagement. Married or married

In terms of health, the mind is bright and strong.

Support Days: 4 Jun., 8 Jun., 12 Jun., 16 Jun., 20 Jun., 24 Jun., 28 Jun.
Lucky Days: 9 Jun., 21 Jun.
Misfortune Days: 10 Jun., 22 Jun.
Bad Days: 1 Jun., 3 Jun., 13 Jun., 15 Jun., 25 Jun., 27 Jun.

Month 6 in the Snake Year (7 Jul 25 - 6 Aug 25)

This month, the life path of the Dragon people moves to a friendly energy line. Therefore, this month's work is full of energy. In terms of work, it is a bright and prosperous path. You will find a patron who will be both a consultant and a helper. During this period, you should use your intelligence and know how to use technology to help. This will result in a good response. Therefore, the most important thing you should do during this period is to take out capital to invest according to the plan or project that you have set. This month is a golden period for investment because there are few obstacles and people are supporting you. Therefore, you should not let this good opportunity pass you by without doing anything. During this period, you will receive useful advice for your work and business.

This month, your finances will still have a good income. Working hard during this period will be worth the effort. The more you do, the more you get. Cash flow will flow in from many sources. There will also be an opportunity to reap the benefits from what you have previously invested.

The family will be peaceful. Members will love and be harmonious.

As for love, for those who already have a lover or partner, during this period, love will be sweet. Your lover will be attentive to you until those around you are jealous.

In terms of physical health, during this period, there will be no illnesses. However, this month, when using the road and traveling, do not be impatient. You still have to be careful about accidents.

Support Days: 2 Jul., 6 Jul., 10 Jul., 14 Jul., 18 Jul., 22 Jul., 26 Jul., 30 Jul.
Lucky Days: 3 Jul., 15 Jul., 27 Jul.
Misfortune Days: 4 Jul., 16 Jul., 28 Jul.
Bad Days: 7 Jul., 9 Jul., 19 Jul., 21 Jul., 31 Jul.

Month 7 in the Snake Year (7 Aug 25 - 6 Sep 25)

This month, your horoscope receives auspicious power from the auspicious constellations that orbit to help spread their influence, thus helping to dissolve the power of misfortune and darkness to fade away.

In terms of work or business, you will find a path of progress and prosperity again. Therefore, you should be diligent and determined to do the work you are responsible for. Work under smooth time to produce the most results and make the highest sales. What you should do on this occasion is to move forward and seize the good opportunities that come during this period. Start working hard to create results and make new sales. Collaboration and investment in various areas are in good shape this month.

This month, the sky opens the way for you. Income will flow from many sources according to what you have invested. You should allocate a portion for saving gold or investing for the future. Within the family, there will be peace, and family members will have better relationships.

In terms of love, this is a time of sweet honey. Lovers are still indulgent. It is a good time for some couples to use this time to sit and talk and clear up problems between each other.

In terms of health, be careful of not getting enough rest, which will cause illness. You must also be careful of heart disease, gastritis, and intestinal inflammation.

Support Days: 3 Aug., 7 Aug., 11 Aug., 15 Aug., 19 Aug., 23 Aug., 27 Aug., 31 Aug.
Lucky Days: 8 Aug., 20 Aug.
Misfortune Days: 9 Aug., 21 Aug.
Bad Days: 2 Aug., 12 Aug., 14 Aug., 24 Aug., 16 Aug.

Month 8 in the Snake Year (8 Sep 25 - 7 Oct 25)
This month, the life path of those born in the year of the Horse is moving to encounter conflicting forces, causing the horoscope to decline. Unevenness will occur from time to time. On this occasion, what you should do is find time to worship the Buddha, make merit, or make donations. In addition, you should keep your mouth shut and do your best. Do not challenge or act prominently to reduce the conflicting forces because there are envious people who are looking for an opportunity to harm you. This month, your financial fate will be in a state of losing money. Be careful of unexpected expenses. Consider signing contracts or hiring jobs carefully. Be careful of being cheated. Starting a new job or investing

during this time should be avoided for now. Do not lend money or sign financial guarantees. Do not do illegal business. In terms of love, there will often be disagreements. Therefore, please be patient. Do not take small matters to heart. Do not interfere in other people's family matters. Do not get involved in entertainment venues or service establishments. This month, there will often be arguments within the home. Be careful of subordinates or servants causing trouble. Be careful that you will have to spend money to repair existing things or you may fall for the tricks of scammers. You must be more careful. Also, you must take care of the health and safety of your family members. Travel horoscope still has dangers. Be careful not to drink and drive and be careful of accidents from tools and equipment while working.

Health is not good. Be careful of allergies and food poisoning.

Relatives and friends are not good during this period. You may have to distance yourself. Be careful of being tricked or slandered by people close to you.

Support Days: 4 Sep., 8 Sep., 12 Sep., 16 Sep., 20 Sep., 24 Sep., 28 Sep.
Lucky Days: 1 Sep., 13 Sep., 25 Sep.
Misfortune Days: 2 Sep., 14 Sep., 26 Sep.
Bad Days: 5 Sep., 7 Sep., 17 Sep., 19 Sep., 29 Sep.

Month 9 in the Snake Year (8 Oct 25 - 6 Nov 25)

This month, evil stars are moving into the horoscope house, so your work and business will encounter chaos again. On this occasion, what you should do is be careful of those who are two-faced and try to slander or secretly attack you. Every activity you will do has a chance of causing trouble. You should avoid confrontation. When making contracts and work documents, you should check the details. Be careful of hidden things that will cause you to be at a disadvantage. Also, be careful of subordinates or servants making mistakes that will cause you to suffer damages. Starting a new job, investing in stocks, and investing in various things should be avoided for now.

Your financial luck is in a state of losing money, so you must remind yourself not to spend more than necessary. Do not gamble, take risks, or act as a guarantor for anyone. Do not do immoral or illegal business.

In terms of family, be careful of accidents that will cause family members to suffer injuries and bleeding. You must also be careful of having problems with neighbors that may cause you to not look at each other.

In terms of love, the person you like is still playing hard to get, so do not be quick to ask for love during this period. Take care of yourself and maintain consistency. Those who already have a family should avoid getting involved with other people's husbands and wives. Be careful that a drop of honey will spread and become a big deal. Do not go to entertainment venues.

Health is not good at this time. Be careful of food poisoning and joint pain in the body. Also, you should not be careless with accidents both at work and while traveling.

Support Days: 2 Oct., 6 Oct., 10 Oct., 14 Oct., 18 Oct., 22 Oct., 26 Oct., 30 Oct.
Lucky Days: 7 Oct., 19 Oct., 31 Oct.
Misfortune Days: 8 Oct., 20 Oct.
Bad Days: 1 Oct., 11 Oct., 13 Oct., 23 Oct., 25 Oct.

Month 10 in the Snake Year (7 Nov 25 - 6 Dec 25)
This month, your horoscope will be smoother and brighter after passing the clashing energy line. Although conflicts will decrease and you will find patrons in your business, the aftermath of problems and difficulties will remain. What you should do during this period is to work honestly and without listening to objections. You should also strengthen good relationships with those you have to contact for business and always make friends with customers and business partners. This will be

very beneficial to you. Although the results are not clear today, the future will be bright. Therefore, you should diligently seek knowledge and improve your lacking skills. Hurry up and solve any remaining obstacles so that you don't have to worry. As for starting a new job, investing, and making investments, you can do this during this period.

In terms of finances, when the business wheels start turning and everything is ready, your income and finances this month will be complete. However, if it is money from luck, be careful because it can easily run out if you are too greedy. It is better to avoid gambling and taking risks. Also, you should not invest in businesses that are at risk of breaking the law.

The family horoscope during this period has auspicious wealth stars, so it is considered another auspicious month. There is a chance to move into a new house or receive good news.

Love is smooth. For singles who have made up their minds, you can ask for love or propose to your lover this month. It is a time when lovers will soften their hearts and agree.

In terms of health, it is good.

Support Days: 3 Nov., 7 Nov., 11 Nov., 15 Nov., 19 Nov., 23 Nov., 27 Nov.
Lucky Days: 12 Nov., 24 Nov.
Misfortune Days: 1 Nov., 13 Nov., 25 Nov.
Bad Days: 4 Nov., 6 Nov., 16 Nov., 18 Nov., 28 Nov., 30 Nov.

Month 11 in the Snake Year (7 Dec 25 - 4 Jan 26)
The road of life is moving into a friendly month. With the support of auspicious stars, all obstacles are reduced. What you should do now is, if there are any plans or projects that have not been implemented in the past month, you can push them to take shape during this period. Because it will appear as a satisfactory income.

For the direction of work and trade during this period, even though there will be changes, it is a better direction. However, you will still have to face the problem of conflicts with people that are not easy to end. You should handle it carefully. As for starting work or entering into stocks, including investing in various things, this month you can proceed and will receive good returns as desired.

This month's financial fortune, even though the path is brighter than before, the more diligent you are, the more likely you are to earn money. But there are still many accumulated expenses. You must be careful of unexpected expenses that will interfere with your liquidity. Therefore, no matter what, you must manage your spending carefully during this period.

The family is loving and harmonious. It is also an auspicious time when there may be a new member.

Love is in a state of competition. There may be a third party. Therefore, if you truly love and want to get married, this month you should hurry to approach and send your elders to ask for your hand in marriage.

In terms of health, there are not many illnesses to bother you.

Support Days: 1 Dec., 5 Dec., 9 Dec., 13 Dec., 17 Dec., 21 Dec., 25 Dec., 29 Dec.
Lucky Days: 6 Dec., 18 Dec., 30 Dec.
Misfortune Days: 7 Dec., 19 Dec., 31 Dec.
Bad Days: 10 Dec., 12 Dec., 22 Dec., 24 Dec.

Amulet for The Year of the Dragon
"The Triple Gem Bodhisattva"

Those born in the Year of the Horse this year should set up and worship the sacred object "Phra Trirattana Bodhisattva" to enhance their destiny. Place it on your work desk or cash desk to ask for the power and authority of the three deities to help eliminate obstacles, problems, dangers, and losses that will occur this year. Bring only good fortune, prosperity, and auspiciousness to the person of destiny.

In one chapter of the Advanced Feng Shui, it was mentioned that the deities who will descend to reside in the Mie Keng (House of Destiny) of the year are deities who can bring both good and bad fortune to the person of destiny in that year. Therefore, worshiping to enhance your destiny with the deities who descend to reside in the same year as your birth year is considered to have the best results and the most impact on you. To use the power of that deity to help protect you while your destiny is declining and having bad karma to alleviate it. At the same time, ask for blessings from them to help your business and trade run smoothly as desired, and bring glory and prosperity to you and your family. Those born in the Year of the Horse or Mie Keng (House of Destiny) are in the sign of Singh.

This year is considered a neutral year for you, not too risky or too up and down. This is because in the horoscope both good stars support you and sometimes there are bad stars that bother you.

Overall, auspicious stars will give you patrons, more honor and fame, and people will respect you. Your work and business will proceed smoothly and progressively. If the owner of the horoscope diligently makes merit and does good deeds, it will support you to meet even more auspicious things. And the auspicious stars will support you to have more opportunities for better work and business. Within the family, there will be happy things and auspicious things. But because in the horoscope bad stars are bothering you, you have to be careful about communicating with people and your emotions. Do not be too impulsive or hot-headed. It will cause chaos and suffering from small things to become big things. In terms of fortune and finance, there will be unnecessary expenses that will cause you to lose money. Even though you have a lot of income, there will also be many losses. And you have to be careful of subordinates or servants causing trouble. A suitable love for those who are still single may be hard to find this year.

In terms of health, there are no serious problems, but you should be careful of heart disease and injuries to your arms and legs. Therefore, if you want to enhance the power of the auspicious stars and resolve disasters, you should set up and worship the sacred object of "Phra Trirattana Bodhisattva" to request the power and authority of the three deities to help your business and trade progress and flourish, have more wealth, be safe from bad things and inauspicious things, have positions and followers to support you, and be free from problems and chaos. The three "Phra Trirattana Bodhisattva" (Thep Sampo) include "Phra Avalokiteshvara Bodhisattva" as the principal Buddha image in the middle. To his left is "Phra Bodhisattva Manjusri" (Bun Chu Pho Sak), the one who excels in wisdom. To his right is "Phra Bodhisattva Samantabhadra" (Pho Eang Pho Sak), the one who excels in beautiful conduct. All three of them are honored as great Bodhisattvas who have a great determination to save beings from suffering. Therefore, if the person with a horoscope has the opportunity to invite "Phra Triratna Bodhisattva" placed in the house or workplace will help to receive the mercy and grace of the three deities to help overcome obstacles and disasters. It will create more auspicious wealth and property. The work and business will be smooth and progress as desired.

In addition, those born in the year of the Horse should wear a sacred pendant of "Phra Triratna Bodhisattva" around their neck or carry it with them when traveling outside the house, whether near or far, so that the person will be filled with auspicious wealth and properties. They will have prosperity and progress in their business and trade. The family will be peaceful and happy throughout the year. It will create better and faster efficiency and effectiveness than before.

Good Direction: Southeast, West, and North
Bad Direction: Northwest
Lucky Colors: Red, Pink, Orange, White, and Yellow.
Lucky Times: 07.00 – 08.59, 15.00 – 16.59, 17.00 – 18.59.
Bad Times: 01.00 – 02.59, 05.00 – 06.59, 19.00 – 20.59.

Good Luck For 2025

Made in the USA
Las Vegas, NV
04 January 2025

15810743R00046